About the Book

On a dark night three teenagers drove along a country road on their way home. Suddenly they noticed strange red and white lights silently gliding by in the black sky above them.

What was this strange object floating toward them?

William Wise, author of *Monsters of the Deep* and *Monsters of North America,* once again tells the provocative story of a group of unknown "monsters" and the people who have witnessed them. Richard Cuffari contributes his dramatic and forceful illustrations to this exciting account of UFO's.

Weekly Reader Books presents

Monsters from Outer Space?

by William Wise/illustrated by Richard Cuffari

G. P. Putnam's Sons/New York

Text copyright © 1978 by William Wise
Illustrations copyright © 1978 by Richard Cuffari
All rights reserved. Published simultaneously in
Canada by Longman Canada Limited, Toronto.
PRINTED IN THE UNITED STATES OF AMERICA

Library of Congress Cataloging in Publication Data
Wise, William.
Monsters from outer space?
SUMMARY: Explains that most sightings of unidenti-
fied flying objects are actually understandable phenomena
and discusses the possibility of intelligent life existing
elsewhere in the universe.
1. Flying saucers—Juvenile literature. [1. Flying
saucers] I. Cuffari, Richard, 1925- II. Title.
TL789.W56 1978   001.9'42   77-16504
ISBN 0-399-61089-8 lib. bdg.

To Deborah, Rebecca, and Gideon

One dark night several years ago, three teen-age girls were driving home along a narrow country road. Looking up at the sky, they saw some red and white lights traveling toward them. At first they thought the lights were part of an airplane.

The lights were so near the ground though, that as the "plane" flew closer, the girls became frightened and their motor stalled. Then the headlights went off, leaving them in complete darkness.

By now the mysterious "flying object" was overhead. It seemed to be made of metal. But it didn't look like any plane or helicopter the girls had ever seen. And when they listened, there was no sound of a motor in the sky.

For a few minutes the object floated above the road. The girls had the feeling it was watching them. Then it turned and glided away. Soon the radio began to play again. The headlights came on. And the motor started without trouble.

When the girls got back to town they told people what had happened. Before long, local newspapers printed the story of their adventure. The papers said the girls had seen a UFO—an *U*nidentified *F*lying *O*bject. But what that object really had been, the papers could not say.

During recent years, many other UFOs have been reported in different parts of the world. Some have been observed at night, others during the day. Some UFOs were said to be round, some flat, and some were said to be large, cigar-shaped objects. Some UFOs were seen by people on the ground, while others were seen by experienced pilots, flying high above the Earth.

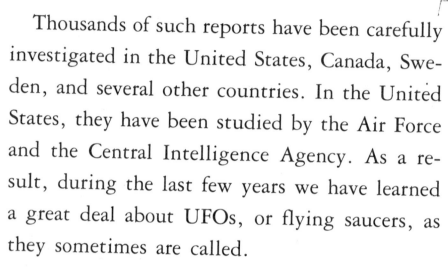

Thousands of such reports have been carefully investigated in the United States, Canada, Sweden, and several other countries. In the United States, they have been studied by the Air Force and the Central Intelligence Agency. As a result, during the last few years we have learned a great deal about UFOs, or flying saucers, as they sometimes are called.

Today we know that a certain number of UFOs are only hoaxes, that is, made-up stories. Some people do this to call attention to themselves. They claim they have seen a space ship, or a flying saucer, and hope they will get their photograph in a newspaper or be invited to be on television.

We also know that sometimes people *think* they have seen a flying object, when it only exists in their imagination. We say that such people have suffered from an hallucination.

In one famous case, a man actually believed that he had seen and climbed aboard a flying saucer. He thought he had flown through the air and talked with the strange-looking occupants of the space ship. But the adventure was just an hallucination, which only had taken place in the man's mind.

It would be a mistake, though, to believe that all UFOs are either hoaxes or hallucinations. The truth is that most UFOs are something else—they are what we call "optical illusions." An optical illusion is something we believe we have seen, when in reality we have seen something quite different. According to United States experts, at least nine out of ten UFOs really are optical illusions, which can be explained by scientific facts.

At times there seems to be almost no limit to the different ways that an optical illusion may occur. Many UFOs are natural objects that people have looked at in the sky, but have mistaken for something else. To the human eye, the planet Venus usually looks like a bright star. But when Venus is close to the horizon, it sometimes appears to be moving back and forth —although it really isn't—and then people may think they have been watching the light of a distant space ship.

Each year, too, numerous shooting stars, or meteors, enter the atmosphere around the Earth. Such shooting stars are made up of gas and small particles of dust or other matter. On entering the atmosphere, they grow extremely hot and burn up. When people see a flight of shooting stars racing across the night sky, they often are deceived into thinking they have seen a formation of lighted space ships flying overhead.

The human eye can be deceived in many other ways. Sometimes light reflecting on a windowpane, or on our eyeglasses, will change the appearance of an object we are looking at. Sometimes sunlight, or a distant searchlight, will strike a bank of clouds. Then, if we happen to be looking at the sky, we may spot moving

shapes which seem to act like flying saucers.

During recent years, too, thousands of man-made objects have been sent into space. Many of them still are circling the Earth. Numerous rockets and communications satellites are now in the sky. Sometimes when they are visible at night, or on a cloudy day, they are mistaken for flying saucers.

Huge weather balloons also are circling our planet. The smallest are a hundred feet wide. When sunlight or bright moonlight strikes a giant balloon, its sides will reflect light in various ways, and the balloon may be mistaken for a mysterious, silent space ship. It probably was such a balloon that the three frightened girls saw floating above the dark country road, the night they were driving home.

Optical illusions may occur just as easily during the day as at night. A number of years ago an American naval officer was driving along a highway in broad daylight with his wife and two children. All at once they saw a group of twelve or fourteen strange white objects flying across the eastern sky. The objects did not look like anything they ever had seen before.

The officer stopped the car, took out his 16-millimeter movie camera, and for several minutes photographed what he thought were either a new kind of airplane or a flight of space ships. He was sure the objects were large and were flying high above the Earth, perhaps as high as 50,000 feet.

But the sunlight, or an unusual condition in the atmosphere, had fooled the officer and his family. For when the films were developed and studied by experts, it turned out that the objects had not been planes or flying saucers after all. Instead they had been merely a flight of birds—probably sea gulls—flying only 2,000 or 3,000 feet away.

People in an airplane can be deceived as easily as people on the ground. In one case, while flying at night, the pilot and co-pilot of a passenger plane caught sight of a dull-red object that seemed to be approaching them at great speed. Just when the plane and the UFO appeared ready to collide, the UFO "turned" slightly, zoomed past the plane, and disappeared into the clouds above.

Afterward the two pilots described the UFO. They said it was shaped like a cigar, was 100 feet long, and had two rows of lighted windows. There was a blue glow underneath it, and a long, red-orange flame behind. Surely a mysterious space ship—until scientists studied the report and decided that the UFO actually had been an unusually bright meteor, traveling far, far away from the pilots and their plane.

Since there are so many ways that our eyes can be deceived by what is in the sky, it is hardly surprising that a certain number of UFOs cannot be completely explained. As a result, many people think that at least a few of these unexplained UFOs are neither optical illusions, nor hoaxes, nor hallucinations. Rather, they believe that we are not the only living creatures in the universe, and that a number of UFOs really are space ships, sent to Earth from other worlds a great distance away.

Curiously enough, such ideas are far from new. Three or four hundred years ago, people first discovered how to use small telescopes to study the heavens. They learned that our planet, Earth, is only one of several planets traveling around the Sun. And so they began to wonder whether there might not be other crea-

tures besides ourselves—perhaps dangerous monsters—living somewhere in space.

Before long, people began to think there may be such space creatures. One early astronomer wrote that although the Sun was very hot, he was certain there were special "Sun people" who were able to live there.

Another early scientist said that a race of large, hideous insects inhabited the Moon. And a third famous philosopher claimed that the people on the planet Mars looked much like us, except that their faces were half black and half yellow. He said this was true, because one evening some Martians had paid him a visit, and told him about life on their planet.

Today, of course, we know much more about our solar system than people did during earlier times. We know there are no creatures like ourselves living on the Sun, the Moon, or Mars. Nor are there any monsters living there either. This does not mean, however, that there might not be *some* form of life on Mars. Nor does it mean that intelligent creatures might not exist somewhere else in the vast universe.

Within the last few years we have sent a number of unmanned spacecraft to the Moon and to several of the planets. Such craft carry many scientific instruments into space. When a spacecraft draws close to a planet, or when it lands there, its instruments begin to send back

information and photographs to scientists on Earth. In part because of such space probes, scientists no longer believe it possible that there are advanced forms of life on Mercury, Venus, Mars, or on any other planet in our solar system.

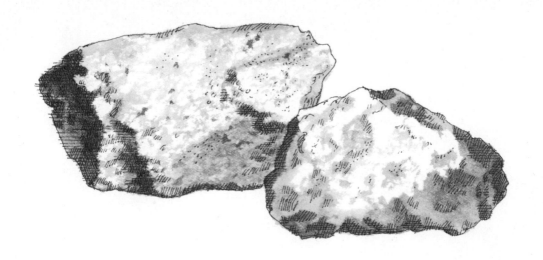

During recent years, too, we have done something that people in earlier times always dreamed of—we have built a manned spacecraft and sent the first travelers to the Moon. After landing safely there, our astronauts were able to collect rocks and other materials. Then they brought back these invaluable specimens to our scientists on Earth. Now we understand far more about the Moon, and about our own planet, than we ever did before.

During recent years, too, better telescopes and other instruments have helped scientists to study the mysteries of distant space. Today we know many new things about the universe and about the countless stars that exist far beyond our solar system.

We know that our Sun is really only an average-size star, and that it is but one of billions of similar stars in the universe. We also know that our entire solar system forms just a tiny part of the matter that exists in space. And we know, too, how great a distance separates us from the nearest stars, and how very long it would take for any spacecraft to reach Earth from another solar system

Distances in space are so enormous that sometimes it is hard for us to understand them. Usually we measure such distances in a special way. The fastest airplane travels 2,000 or 3,000 miles an hour. A spacecraft travels 25,000 miles an hour. To reach Centaurus, the star system closest to Earth, it would have to travel through space for about 120,000 years.

But a beam of light travels much, much faster than a space ship can. It travels 186,000 miles every *second*. Moving at the speed of light, a space ship would have to travel four and a half years before reaching Centaurus. So we say that such a star system is four and a half light-years away from Earth. And some stars in the universe are millions of times farther from us than Centaurus is.

Because such great distances separate us from even the nearest stars, most scientists do not believe that creatures from other worlds really have visited the Earth in mysterious space ships or have landed here in strange-looking flying saucers. Yet many scientists *do* believe that intelligent creatures might be living somewhere else in space.

A few years ago, while using giant radio telescopes, some astronomers received puzzling radio signals from far beyond our solar system. They called the signals "LGM"—for Little Green Men—because it was possible that some kind of living creatures were sending the signals in our direction.

Since then we have learned that such radio signals are emitted by a special kind of star, called a pulsar, and that they are not being sent by living beings. This does not mean, of course, that there are no other forms of life in the universe, or that we ourselves are the only living creatures in all of space.

Many scientists believe that although we have not yet located them, there probably are a number of other solar systems like our own, somewhere in the universe. They believe that there may be planets like Earth, and that some kind of intelligent creatures could be living there.

Each year we learn more and more about space and the universe. As a result, one day we may be able to send our astronauts to Mars or

build a permanent space-station on the Moon.
And perhaps in a hundred or two hundred
years, travelers will leave Earth to visit a distant
star or another solar system.

One day, too, we may discover a solar system
similar to our own in distant space. If that
should happen, we may find that there really
are other intelligent creatures living in the universe and that although they are very different
from ourselves, they are as eager to communi-
cate with us as we are with them.